How To Grow A Vegetable Garden

How To Grow A Vegetable Garden

JAMES DOWNIE

How To Grow A Vegetable Garden

See other books by the Author at his Amazon author page:
www.amazon.com/author/bestselling

Published by Blue Peg Publishing

If you have purchased the ebook version of this book, then please consider buying the print version if your family enjoys the ebook.

Contents

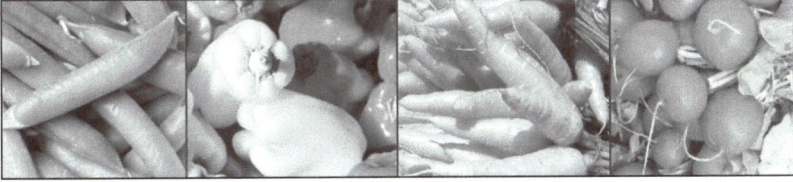

CHAPTER 1

Getting Back To Basics By Growing Your Own Vegetables

Your vision of hand-picking and lovingly preparing fresh vegetables from your backyard garden can easily become a reality.

In the same amount of time you now spend maintaining your lawn, and for less money, you can turn your personal property into a thriving source of healthy food.

Embracing vegetable gardening will ultimately make you feel richer, healthier, happier, and more connected to our fascinating, living planet.

There is a voluntary simplicity to creating a life where you grow what you eat.

As we work to enhance the health and fertility of our earth, we find our own health and creativity calmly growing in unison. We have a basic touchstone to our planet and that is reassuring in a world that is becoming increasing complex and challenging.

Reaching this dimension of contentment and self-satisfaction is as vital as the size of the zucchini or pumpkin you will harvest in the fall.

This book will help you make it happen.

Chapter by chapter, we will illustrate how you can reduce your family grocery bill by up to 70 per cent with your homegrown harvest.

We'll show you how your garden can enhance your family life and your own sense of well-being.

In the upcoming chapters, you will get a common sense guide to the world of vegetable gardening. It will give you many options for getting engaged in this gardening world, so that you can pick and choose the commitment you feel will work best for you.

This book approaches gardening from the point of view of fitting it into the time and space of your life. Instead of alphabetical plant listings with accompanying growing seasons and growing facts, it groups garden crops together in a series of projects.

You can start and end with one single chapter, a salad garden in your yard or patio. When you have mastered that and it fits and enhances your daily agenda, you can move on to creating a garden of vegetable staples, and then move to more complex crops and finally to spreading plants that are rewarding to eat, but take more time and space to grow.

Sandwiched in to brighten your gardening journey are tips and techniques to save you both time and money and make the most of your gardening efforts.

Gardening should be a genuine pleasure in your life, a rewarding pastime that lightens your step and enhances your family meals. It should not be a burden that makes your daily agenda even more complicated and gobbles all your weekend recreational time.

The tales of extreme gardening we hear are enough to make many people postpone its pleasures until retirement, when they believe they will finally have the time. That is a genuine shame, because when we are at our busiest and most stressed, that is when we really need the voluntary simplicity of a little bit of "time out" to garden.

The best advice we can offer from the start is to begin small and grow your vegetable garden as you grow yourself, expanding slowly to new areas of interest and expertise until you have perfected your approach.

Start with the quickest and fastest reward for your time and money, a salad garden. Then add staples like peas and beans and for a bit of fun, some corn. Grow into stalwarts like cabbage and cauliflower and broccoli, and if you are ready, go for the whole gusto and sow some pumpkin and squash just to have fun with them.

Add fragrant and beautiful herbs for flavourings and their healthy side effects and pretty soon you will create an ongoing and free flow of nutritious vegetables to your dinner table. With easy preservation methods like freezing, you can also enjoy the fruits of your summer labour all year long.

If your backyard or patio area is insufficient and you still long for a chance to work the good earth, check with your local town hall to see if there are options for community gardens. These are usually cordoned off areas available for community gardeners to rent for a nominal fee or in some cases, to work free provided you grow a few extra rows for the local food bank or soup kitchen.

In the practical advice that follows, there will be techniques to prepare the soil and how and when to start your vegetables.

We will not only focus on what to do, but in our myths and mistakes collection, we will talk about some common beginner mistakes and how you can avoid them.

We will create a simple gardening year schedule that keeps you close to your hobby all seasons, but ensures it does not become a burden at any one time. We'll give you the resources to ensure that your crop selection and growing times exactly match your specific climate zone and growing season.

Add to that a smattering of cherished recipes and vegetable storage ideas to make the most of your harvest and you are well on the road to a new gardening experience.

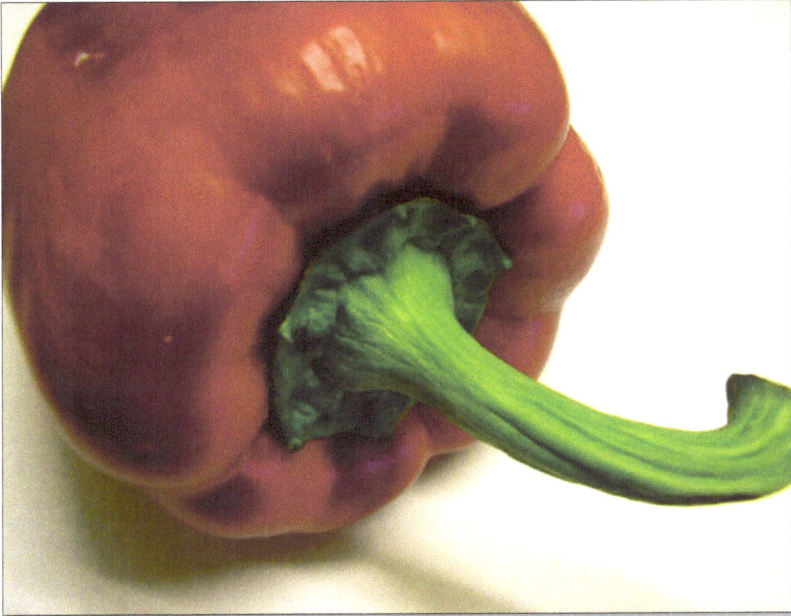

Red Pepper

Your Budget Savings Start Here

As we suggested at the start, a backyard vegetable garden can reduce your family grocery bill by up to 70 per cent.

There are other significant benefits as well.

A wealth of fresh vegetables prompts families to eat less meat. Meat is frequently the most expensive item in your grocery cart. Even having meatless meals a couple of nights a week reduce your food expenditures.

Additional savings come from using fewer garbage bags and plastics because your waste is composted.

If you are concerned about the health impact of eating chemically-laden and genetically modified food, you can embrace growing your food organically.

Benefits Extend Beyond The Pocketbook

Gardening is one of the most beneficial practices you can engage in for the betterment of your health.

Backyard gardeners often report a general sense of well being when they get involved in growing things. There is s sense of escape from the chaos of the modern world when you are calmly weeding a garden or harvesting a crop.

Gardeners talk about the pleasure they experience from feeling connected to all of life when they are working in their garden.

Science supports the concept that those who feel akin to nature are healthier and happier.

Harvard naturalist and Pulitzer Prize winner Edward O. Wilson, creator of the term "biophilia" (Iover of living things), says he believes we have an affinity with nature because we are part of it. That translates to us preferring to look at growing things rather than concrete and steel.

As part of the natural world, we find ourselves connected to it and restored by it.

Some studies have shown that the health benefits of being close to nature can lower blood pressure, boost immune function and reduce stress.

Families Growing Together

Growing your own vegetable garden also teaches youngsters about the original sources of food and turns them away from over-processed, unhealthy diet choices.

Detractors of gardening suggest that it is too much work in our hectic lives. The reality is that gardening is a lot of fun and a source of play in the fresh air for modern families. Children and parents both delight in watching the process of growth.

The sharing of chores and meals cooked from a fresh vegetable harvest is a bond that brings many families closer together. In tending our gardens, it is said, we often tend ourselves.

Vegetable gardens are also vehicles to teach our children more about life. One gardener said the day she planted her first potato was when she heard her two children arguing about whether or not French fries came from a tree. Neither one knew which vegetable they came from.

Rise In Popularity

With all these benefits, it is little wonder that vegetable gardening is more popular now than it has ever been.

American First Lady Michelle Obama created a garden on the grounds of the White House in Washington. People were so intrigued at the idea of President Barack Obama and his family growing vegetables that a book called "American Grown: The Story of The White House Kitchen Garden and Gardens Across America" was produced as a charity project.

The First Lady's humour in poking fun at her failures as much as her successes makes the idea of gardening all the more approachable to those of us with varying degrees of skill. She wrote that she grew only five pumpkins in three years and produced perfectly shaped but tasteless cantaloupes.

All of our sudden, our misshapen cucumbers don't seem to be such a worry.

Of course gardening has long been a great hobby of world leaders. Currently Prince Charles is world-famous for his scrupulously maintained gardens and 350 farmed acres at his Highgrove residence.

Thomas Jefferson, a former president of the United States, wrote in a 1785 letter that "cultivators of the earth are the most valuable citizens. They are the most vigorous, the most independent, the most virtuous, and they are tied to their country and wedded to its liberty and interests by the most lasting bands."

So what are we waiting for?

Let's get back to basics and grow our own vegetables.

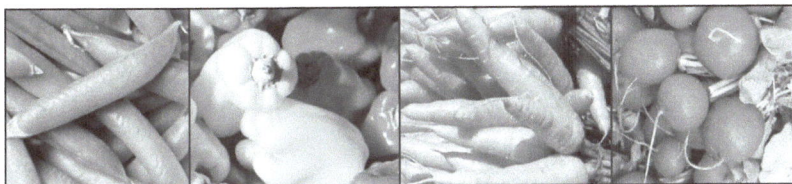

CHAPTER 2

Nurturing Your Soil For Biggest And Best Results

Radish

Growing a vegetable garden is a lifestyle choice that has the added benefit of helping you build a closer connection to this world we live in and understanding all its cycles and adapting to them.

One of the essential decisions you need to make at the beginning is whether or not you wish to grow your vegetables organically.

The organic gardening philosophy is simply that you feed and care for the soil, and it in turn, will feed and care for your plants. Completing the cycle, your plants will then feed and care for you, and the rhythm continues indefinitely.

For the beginning gardener, you may decide you want to start growing organically from the start. Others may wish to learn more about it and make a choice after they have mastered the basics.

As long as you garden with respect for the earth in which you plant, you will be rewarded with a good harvest.

In this book we will designate the different areas in which you would need to consider options if you chose to grow organically. Otherwise, all the basics of getting started and growing a great garden will apply.

Either way, though your dream is to be harvesting great baskets of fresh crops, your reality is you must start by carefully planning your garden and preparing the soil.

Talking the first step to a bountiful vegetable garden means walking out into your backyard or designated plot and looking at it as if you are seeing for the first time. You have to begin to feel how this land is going to impact on you and the crops you want to grow.

Bring a notebook and jot down your observations. Is your backyard sloped or flat? Are their marshy areas or is it high and dry. Is it sunny or shady or a mixture of both?

Is there an area that is more weed-filled than in other places? That is likely where the soil is the worst.

Consider all the areas of your land you have to use for a garden, whether it is a front, side or back yard or a plot of land in another location, and study it carefully. Does it have maximum sunlight, or is it shaded by trees, sheds or houses most of the morning and afternoon?

Study the patterns of the sun and record the number of hours you can depend that it will shine directly on your garden.

Ideally, if you have a spot near your house in full sunlight, you are halfway to success. You already have a prime factor for growth, the sunlight, and you have the convenience of being able to tend your garden daily, even if you just have a few minutes. You will also be in a position to frequently monitor any pests and deal with them before they take control of a crop.

Study the potential site again to see if there are any drainage issues for plants since vegetables are not happy when their feet are frequently in the water. The best time to look for drainage issues is after a heavy rainstorm. See how fast the land is drained or whether pools of water last for hours or even days.

Now consider the air movement in your potential site. You need to allow summer's gentle breezes to blow through your garden, but you do not want to be on top of an extremely windy hill, for example, where unrelenting winds will dry out your plants and break them.

Does your potential garden spot have a source for watering? If it is in your yard, can you hook up a garden hose or makeshift irrigation system? If you are using a plot of land you have access to in the nearby countryside, will you have to bring water from town, or is there a natural source?

If there is no convenient way to water your garden, consider another site. If you have perfect conditions of rain and sun ratios, you could be all right, but Mother Nature has her quirks and you cannot count on sufficient rain to keep your garden lush for an entire summer.

Preparing The Soil

You may be surprised that the last item mentioned in locating your garden is the health of the soil, but that is because if all other conditions are excellent, you can usually work with your soil to enrich it.

Some gardeners with the perfect location but horrible soil grow magnificent gardens by using raised beds, bringing in the most fertile of soil and growing their crops in large, boxed beds.

What makes good garden soil?

It should be well drained, easily supplied with organic matter like compost, reasonably free of stones and capable of retaining moisture.

When you start to study your soil, dig a hole about 20 inches deep to get an idea of what your subsoil looks like. For example, if you have a bit of dirt but it is on top of a hard rock ledge, it will be difficult for your plants to develop a healthy root system.

Is the top of the soil darker than the bottom? That is a very good sign because it means the top soil has a high organic content.

Moisten the soil until it is pliable. Then scoop up a handful and try to form it into the shape of a breadstick. If it crumbles, that means you have a lot of sand in your soil, and that will need to be fixed.

If it breaks apart after it is about an inch long, it has a small amount of clay, and that is good. If you can build something about the size of a breadstick out of it, you likely have about 50 percent clay, and that needs to be addressed.

Also check your soil for earthworms, since their presence is a sign of healthy, active soil.

If all other aspects of your garden are great, but your soil is poor, there are many ways to improve it. Either by adding organic matter, lime, commercial fertilizer or other materials, you can substantially improve it.

Working The Soil

As anxious as you may be to get started in the spring of the year, do not work the soil when it is very wet. If you put your hands into it and it sticks together in a ball and doesn't easily crumble, go back inside and wait at least another week or two.

Working with wet soil and planting in soil that is too wet will not work. Right from the start, these realities remind us that successful vegetable gardening is as much about patience as it is about skill.

If the soil has been worked before and a previous owner had a garden in the location you are now considering, you may get away with just adding additional organic material or commercial fertilizers.

Of the fertilizers, composted manure is among the most effective. If you decide to add one of the commercially prepared plant food fertilizers, distribute it at about four pounds for every 1,000 square feet. This is not a case of "more is better." If you overuse fertilizer, you will burn your plants.

Likewise, use the dried, commercial manure on your garden. Remember that fresh, hot manure will also burn your plants. If you have access to the latter, be sure to put it in your compost pile before you use it in your garden.

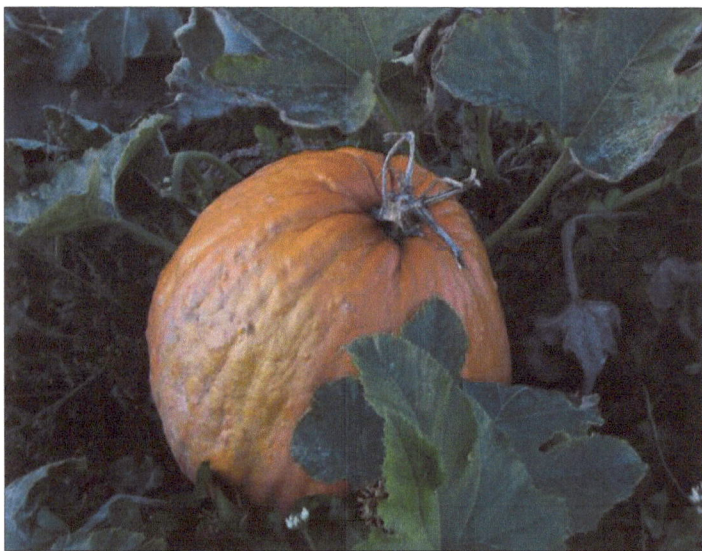

Pumpkin

Planting Is About Science

Once you have tilled your garden site and prepared your soil, or created a raised bed garden filled with healthy soil, you should have the pH of your soil tested. This is a test that tells you if your soil has too much acidity or alkalinity.

Make the sure the ground is dry before you have it tested.

To save yourself money, you can purchase an inexpensive pH test kit at most nurseries. Some garden centres will even test it for you for free as an additional service.

If the pH is lower than 7.0, your soil is high in acid. If it is higher than 7.0, it is high in alkaline. All nurseries carry materials to amend your soil. If you need to raise the pH level, generally lime is used, and if you need to lower it, generally sulfur is used.

As a rule of thumb, add four pounds of lime per 100 square foot of garden for every pH point below 6.5. Add one pound of sulfur per 100 square feet for every pH point above 7.5.

If you are gardening organically, to raise the pH level add ashes of hardwoods, bone meal, crushed marble or crushed oyster shells. To lower the pH level, add sawdust, composted oak leaves, wood chips, peat moss, cottonseed meal or leaf mold.

The best approach is to adjust the pH level in your soil gradually over several gardening seasons.

Before you make major adjustments, sit down and seriously plan your garden and the crops you plan to grow, since different vegetables have different pH requirements. Most vegetables prosper in soils that are slightly acid and can be injured if you apply too much lime. For that reason, only use lime in extreme circumstances when serious adjustment is needed.

If vegetables will be your main crop and your soil is excessively alkaline, you would be better off building a raised planting bed and importing your soil.

Six Steps to Enriching Soil With Compost

If you are growing organically or just interested in reducing your waste and building an effective compost pile in the process, here are six easy steps to getting started.

Compost is organic matter, such as leaves, coffee grinds and egg shells that have been allowed to decompose. There are two kinds of compost materials: brown and green. Browns are things like dried leaves and black and white newsprint. Greens are grass trimmings and kitchen scraps such as egg shells.

There are lots of expensive composting devices on the market, and if you have the budget to purchase a composter they are effective. But you do not need anything more than basic tools and a little time to get started for virtually nothing.

1. Build a base of natural, organic materials for your compost heap. Use coarse, unwieldy materials that don't neatly stack together, because you want air to be able to circulate. Corn stalks are great, for example, as are the hardy stems of old sunflowers and pruned branches.

2. After you build a base, start adding organic matter. Remember the one cardinal rule of composting: You need two parts brown for every one part green.

3. Assemble your compost heap in layers as if you were making lasagna. Make your base of browns and greens, then sprinkle organic soil on top of it, and add a little water. Then start again.

4. The more often you turn your compost pile using your garden fork or shovel, the quicker your added materials will decompose.

5.   Avoid attracting unwanted creatures to your backyard by making sure when you add kitchen scraps that you work them well into the pile and cover them well with organic soil.

6.   It is not necessary to cover your compost pile with a tarp. Instead, if you have heavy rains and you observe the compost is becoming soggy and water-logged, just add more browns. Conversely, if you got through a drought period and your compost pile is becoming too dry, add wet organic materials like freshly mown grass. However, a black tarp is sometimes useful in colder climates to draw the heat and promote decomposition.

Plan Before You Plant

You are nearly ready to get out there and fulfill your goal of growing your own vegetables. There is only one step left, but it is the most important one, and that is planning your garden.

The biggest mistake beginning gardeners make is to be overly-enthusiastic about the amount of time they can commit to maintaining their garden. It cannot be over-emphasized that it is much better to have a small, well-maintained and healthy, productive garden than a sprawling one that is full of weeds.

You may want to ease into vegetable gardening by starting with patio planters of tomatoes, beans and lettuce. You may start with a five by five foot raised garden bed, and expand to a 100 by 100 foot entire backyard spread.

Either way, you will be more inclined to enjoy the experience and have good crops for your efforts if you start small and gradually expand, than if you start large and realize you have taken on too large a task.

There are a few other considerations.

Depending on the wildlife in your area, make sure that your garden is surrounded by a high fence and possibly topped with a mesh to keep out dogs, rabbits, squirrels, chipmunks and other animals.

Green Peppers

Look for areas that will support a trellis for climbing vegetables like beans and peas.

Take time to draw out a diagram of your garden, mapping out what you will plant and where. Most experienced gardeners use an east-west strategy if they are planting in rows, because that leaves your tallest plants growing in the north end and the shorter plants in front to avoid them being shaded.

If you are planting on a hill, make your rows horizontal not vertical so the water won't gush down the rows and take the topsoil with it.

Perennial vegetables like rhubarb and asparagus should be planted to the side of the garden where they won't interfere with tilling and weeding activities.

Group your early producing salad crops like lettuce, spinach, and radishes together and allow for extra space for successive plantings.

When they are done for the season, you can use that space for late-season crops like kale.

Create mounds for sprawling, vining plants like cucumbers and pumpkins.

If you are using a raised bed, keep it narrow enough that you can reach across to weed. If you are planting into the ground, be sure to allow room in your rows for weeding.

It is often helpful to sketch out your potential garden plot before you put even one plant in the ground. Moving the plants on paper is a lot easier than discovering they are in the wrong place in the soil.

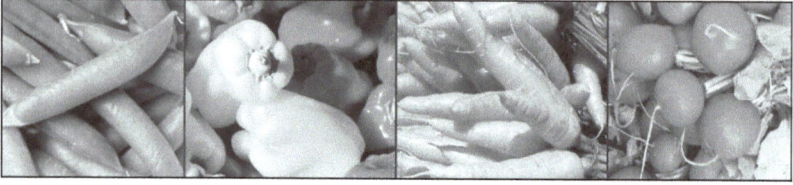

CHAPTER 3

Grow Your Own Salad Vegetables For Quick Gratification

Lettuce grows quickly

For the beginning gardener, the time from planting to harvesting can stretch longingly over the hot days of summer.

By starting with salad vegetables like lettuce, spinach, radish and tomatoes, you will start to feel the gratification for your work earlier. This will heighten your enthusiasm for the long, hot weeks of weeding and maintenance that stretch between you and other crops.

Lettuce

Lettuce grows quite easily and quickly, so the key is to plant just the right amount for your family (it won't keep) and ensure that you have a steady supply.

Remember that the average packet of lettuce contains about 2,000 seeds, so one little packet should take you through the entire season. Sow about 10 to 12 seeds indoors about six weeks before the last frost date and place them under a fluorescent light. Then transplant them to your garden about a month later.

To transplant any vegetables you start inside, simply dig a small hole which is slightly wider and deeper than the root ball of your new plant. Water the plant thoroughly before transplanting it to lessen its shock. Then gently tap the pot to loosen the roots and remove the plant.

Place it gently into the hole slightly deeper than it was growing in the pot, and tap down the soil around it with your fingers. Then water thoroughly.

At the same time you put your transplants into the garden soil, sow about 12 more seeds directly into the soil. Sow lettuce seeds a quarter of an inch deep and one inch apart in your garden.

Most lettuce will sprout in two to eight days when the soil temperature gets to 55 degrees Fahrenheit.

For the duration of summer, sow lettuce once every two weeks to ensure a steady supply. As autumn and the threat of the first frost nears, sow only cold-tolerant varieties like romaines and butterhead.

If you are starting small, you can also grow lettuce successfully on your back deck or patio in long, rectangular containers, again rotating the times the seeds are placed in the soil.

When it comes time to harvest lettuce, pick it in the morning when the leaves are plump and full of water. If you pick lettuce when it is wilting on a hot afternoon, it will not likely survive until suppertime.

Thin your lettuce by pulling leaves to allow space for new leaves to grow. Tear the leaves off gently or use scissors to harvest baby lettuce.

Rinse it thoroughly with cool water, shake off the excess moisture and store the lettuce in plastic bags in the refrigerators.

Keep leaf lettuce trimmed to about six inches apart, romaines to about 10 inches apart, and heading varieties about 12 inches apart.

To reduce the growth of weeds, mulch between your lettuce plants with grass clippings or other organic mulch.

The two biggest pests attacking your lettuce are slugs and aphids. Slug presence is visible when you see smooth-edged holes chewed into the outer leaves. Slugs can be caught in the act most often on days of light rain or drizzle. You can collect them with your gloved hand and get rid of them, or set slug traps for them baited with beer.

Another very effective way to stop slugs is to take any coffee left in your pot and pour it gently over their leaves. Making that part of your morning routine will go a long way to eliminating any slug problem.

Aphids, on the other hand, sometimes descend in groups on the folds between lettuce leaves. You can rinse them away with cool water.

You should not grow lettuce in the same spot in your garden for more than three years. Otherwise, you will likely fall prey to soil borne diseases. The soil where you are growing lettuce should never been allowed to dry out and crack either, if you want your plants to stay healthy.

If your goal is to reduce your grocery bill and enjoy fresh produce, you can start with no better crop than lettuce. By keeping in stock a few salad basics, from olives to dried fruits or fresh berries, to chicken breasts to nuts, you can add one whole meal each day from your garden simply by growing this one crop.

Additionally, you can augment your homemade sandwiches with slices of crisp lettuce and even use it as an edible garnish for trays of meat or devilled eggs.

Lettuce is high in many nutrients, including Vitamin A. Dark leaves have more of that vitamin than pale ones.

Tips

If summer becomes unrelentingly hot just as your head lettuce reaches its peak, construct a shade cloth over it (even an old dishtowel or sheet) to cover it. Water at midday if at all possible if the temperature continues to soar.

Once lettuce looks perfect in the garden, do not leave it there even for an extra day. Its perfection is fleeting, and you need to take full advantage of it when it arrives.

You can save lettuce seeds from any plant since they are open-pollinated. Let some lettuce go past its prime to the point where it gets yellow flowers and then ripe seedpods. Put a support around the plants to keep the heads from falling over.

Gather the dry seeds in a paper bag and crush them with your hands. Sift the seeds to separate the seeds from the chaff. Package and label and store these seeds to start growing inside next spring.

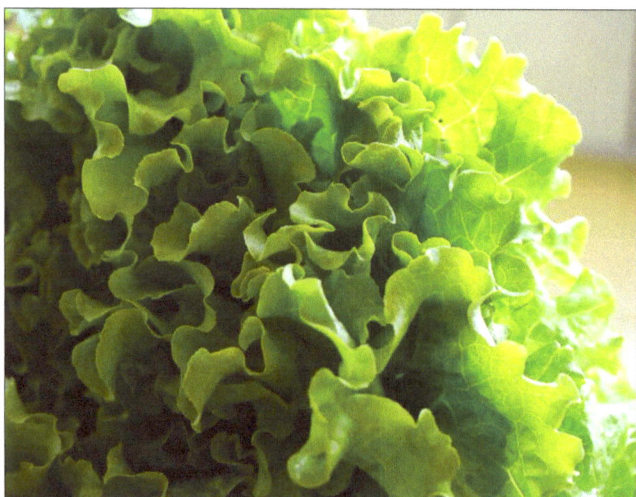

Lettuce

Radish

Another easy to grow vegetable that provides flavour and colour to your salads is the radish. In a rainbow of colours and shapes, radish is a wonderful way to excite children about gardening as well.

Like lettuce, it can be sown continuously throughout the summer to provide a constant supply, since it is best eaten fresh and does not keep well. If you sow it every three weeks, you will have radish for most of the summer.

Plant your radish directly into the ground in the spring, about two weeks before you expect the last spring frost. About three weeks before the first anticipated frost of autumn, only plant rat-tail radish.

Radish likes a bed of loosened soil, about six to 10 inches deep, nicely mixed with well-rotted manure. Sow seeds a half inch deep and an inch apart in rows about one foot apart.

Once they start to grow, thin the radishes to three inches apart. Thin them early, when they have only two or three leaves. This reduces disturbances to the development of nearby plant roots. Oriental radishes need to be about 10 inches apart to have room to grow into their larger size.

You will see the seeds sprouting in three days to a week.

Radishes need full sun, but can benefit from some shade if the summer is very hot. To get them through a heat wave, cover them with a shade cloth of a lightweight material.

In the heat of summer when you go to your garden to harvest your radish, take a bowl of cool water with you. You know your radish is ready to pick when it is bigger than a grape.

Like lettuce, if it looks perfect, pick it, don't wait. Radishes that stay in the ground too long will be ruined. They develop a pithy texture and crack after heavy rains.

As soon as you pull the radish from the ground and remove its leaves using kitchen shears, place it into the cool water.

Radish will keep for about three weeks in the refrigerator. The larger, oriental varieties can be safely left in the ground until the fall and then dug up before the soil freezes.

Use them sliced or grated into a salad or a slaw or layer them in sandwiches. Eat them with breed and butter or braise them in butter to experience their wonderful flavour and texture. You can also substitute diced radishes for water chestnuts in stir-fries.

Radishes are nutritious. They provide vitamin C., fiber, lutein and a range of minerals.

The weather actually impacts the radish's flavor. Radishes grown in an extremely hot summer are usually a bit spicier than those raised in a regular summer.

An extremely cold spring can also impact your radish crop. If they are sown into the ground early and the cold becomes unexpectedly severe and prolonged, some of them will bolt meaning they rush to produce flowers at the expense of developing plump and healthy roots.

They are also susceptible to two main pests: the flea beetles that make small holes in their leaves and cabbage root maggots and cutworms that rasp holes or channels into radish skins.

Creating lightweight floating row covers will protect your radish crop from these intruders.

If you want to save your radish seeds for next year, first check and make sure that you have purchased an open-pollinated variety. If you have, allow about four plants to bloom together and wait for the seed pods to dry and turn brown before you harvest the seeds.

Crush the pods with your hands and then sift them to separate the seeds from the chaff. Store the seeds in a cool, dry place for up to five years.

If you are gardening organically, remember that radishes make a good fall cover crop. Plant them in the soil where you were growing beans, peas, or other nitrogen-fixing legumes and the radishes will utilize the nitrogen left behind in the soil.

Spinach

One of the fastest to grow and most versatile of the vegetable crops is spinach. You can grow the semi-savoyed type with dark leaves that are puckered or the smooth-leafed varieties that are a lighter shade of green and a little easier to wash.

You can pick the leaves when they are just babies and tender to eat fresh in a salad, or you can let it mature and use it as a cooked green or in a variety of dishes from quiche to pizza.

Start the seeds indoors about six weeks before the expected last frost of winter or put them in a protected frame or greenhouse outdoors. After three weeks, plant another group of spinach seeds, and three weeks after that, plant again.

After that, don't plant again until about seven weeks before your first expected fall frost, and then sow one final crop for a fall harvest. If you have a greenhouse or a thick row cover, you can plant winter spinach about four weeks before the expected frost.

Spinach should be planted after the soil is loosened and mixed with an organic fertilizer high in nitrogen such as soybean meal or alfalfa meal. Sow the seeds one-half inch deep and about two inches apart. Leave at least eight inches between the rows to walk.

If you keep the plants too close and crowded together, they will be more likely to develop mildew and have problems with slugs.

Never plant spinach in soil where beets or chard were grown in the previous year. These crops are closely related and play host to the same soil borne diseases.

Gradually thin the plants as they grow so that the leaves of adjacent plants barely touch.

Within six weeks you will be harvesting your crop, pinching off individual leaves but leaving the central rosette alone. If the weather becomes unusually hot, the spinach plant may bolt. If you see that your plants are suddenly developing a tall, central stem, then pick them all to save them. Steam-blanch and freeze the leaves.

Check your crop regularly for leaf miners. Use your fingers to gently remove infested leaves. To keep slugs from eating your spinach leaves, remove mulch and place traps baited with beer.

If some of your crop's new growth seems to be accompanied by the yellowing of older leaves, pull up the plants. Aphids and leafhoppers are also capable of transmitting viral diseases to spinach.

Spinach is just loaded with nutrients for you and your family. Besides vitamins A and C, it has calcium and iron. You can eat it raw in salads and sandwiches, or cooked as a green.

A flexible food, spinach can be included in everything from chocolate cake to quiche to pizza. When you are searching for recipes, remember that any recipe with the word Florentine in its name includes cooked spinach.

Recipe for the Perfect Spinach Quiche

A hit at a country market in the prairie lands of Canada, this fluffy quiche is responsible for more converts to spinach than Popeye the Sailor. The secret, according to the locals, is the mayonnaise, not a common ingredient in other quiches.

Fluffy Quiche

½ cup light mayonnaise 125 ml

½ cup milk 125 ml

4 eggs, lightly beaten

8 ounces shredded, reduced-fat cheddar cheese 250 g

1 ½ cups chopped fresh spinach 375 ml

¼ cup chopping onion 60 ml

1 unbaked pie shell

Method:

Preheat oven to 400 degrees Fahrenheit (200 degrees Celsius).

Line a cookie sheet with foil.

In a large bowl, whisk together mayonnaise and milk until smooth. Whisk in eggs. Layer spinach, cheese, and onion in pie shell, making several layers of each. Pour in egg mixture.

Place quiche on prepared cookie sheet. Cover quiche with foil.

Bake in preheated oven for 45 minutes. Remove cover, and bake 10 to 15 minutes, or until top is golden brown and filling is set.

Tomatoes

Complete your salad garden with either patio containers of tomatoes, or a few plants in your garden.

The single most important thing about growing great tomatoes is to understand that they need eight solid hours of sunlight every day to flourish. If they don't get it, while they may not die, they will be spindly and produce little fruit.

Plant tomatoes in soil that has a pH balance of 5.5 to 6.8 and make sure it is rich in organic matter. The soil needs to be well-drained and able to hold water evenly. If the soil is too moist and the tomatoes' roots constantly wet, they will develop problems like fruit splitting and blossom end rot.

Like so many plants, do not continue to plant your tomatoes in the same spot each year. Many of the diseases that plague them reside in the soil and will just return the following season, stronger than ever.

When it comes time to plant, you have to select from hybrid or heirloom tomatoes. Hybrids are tomatoes whose breeding has been strictly controlled and they are usually more disease resistant. However, heirloom tomatoes often taste better and are open pollinators, handed down from generation to generation.

If you live in an area with a long growing season, you can sow the seeds directly into your garden. In many of the northern parts of the world, however, you need to start the plants indoors for about six weeks before they are stalwart enough to go in the ground.

The joy of growing your own tomatoes from seed is enhanced by the wide variety of tomatoes available to you and the reality that you know exactly what you are getting.

If you buy tomato plants at your local supplier, however, make sure that the leaves are clean and dark green. Plants that have some leaves that are yellow or brown are already stressed and should be avoided.

Wait until all danger of frost has passed before you put any tomatoes in the ground. Place the plants about 24 to 36 inches apart if they are the kind that sprawl on a vine, or about 15 inches if they grow up a trellis.

Be careful not to over-fertilize your tomatoes. Too much nitrogen will give you lots of leaves but very few tomatoes.

Many gardeners spray their tomato leaves about two or three times a week with a kelp solution. It helps them stay disease free.

Plant your tomatoes deep, and on their sides. Remove the lower stems and branches off the tomatoes, leaving only the upper most top leaves. Cover the entire plant with soil, leaving only the top leaves visible.

If cutworms are a huge problem in your garden, place an empty toilet paper roll around the stem of the tomato.

When watering your tomatoes, keep the water towards the base of the plant and keep the leaves dry. Never use an overhead sprinkler to water your tomatoes. Tomatoes can become infected when airborne spores land on wet plants.

Water your tomatoes regularly, but allow the soil to dry between watering.

Remember that particularly hot and dry summers tend to produce thick-skinned tomatoes. That is because the plant is trying to conserve moisture.

Tomatoes can be affected by a number of blights and diseases, all of which are more likely to appear if the plants are too close together or watered incorrectly.

Tomatoes

CHAPTER 4

The Garden Staples
That Stretch Your Budget

Peas

Many things will influence which vegetables you will grow when you establish your garden, but the two considerations of time and space will ultimately settle many decisions for you.

Crops that are delicate to grow in your climate and that need excessive maintenance will be poor choices for the beginning gardener who plans to sandwich a gardening habit into an already full life.

Likewise, an overabundance of sprawling vegetables will not work if you have only a five-foot-by-three foot raised bed garden. In making the tough choices about what to plant, consider what will grow easily, what can be reasonably worked into your family's diet, and what will yield a sizeable crop in limited space.

That's why so many gardens have a row or two of beans and peas, staples that pass every test for practicality and performance.

Peppers are another high yielding crop and are highly versatile when working into your family's meal plan, although they are a little more difficult to grow.

The other staple crop that is so attractive to gardeners, but which requires the luxury of some space, is corn. What is sweeter than to harvest half a dozen ears of fresh corn and cook them for supper that very night?

Like almost everything else, all of these vegetable garden staples do best in well-drained soil that has hours of daily sunshine.

Green Beans

To prepare your soil for a crop of beans, work it eight to 10 inches deep, raking it frequently to break up any large clods of earth. Take out all weeds and rocks.

Your beans will really do better if you fertilize the soil before planting. Spread fertilizer evenly over the area you plan to plant your beans in, and mix it in with the top three to four inches of soil.

There are three varieties of beans, with snap beans being the most popular overall for their versatility in meals. Pinto beans can also be grown, as well as lima beans.

Do not plant your beans until all danger of frost has passed in the spring. If you are planting a second crop for fall, make sure they are in the ground 10 to 12 weeks before the first expected frost.

For bush beans, plant the seeds about one inch deep and two inches apart in a row, with the rows being about 2 ½ feet apart. Once the beans are up, thin them so there the plants are three to four inches apart.

Pole beans should be planted in rows three to four feet apart. Plant them in hills. In the middle of the hill, place a six to eight foot stake. Plant three to four seeds around the stake, about one inch deep in the soil. The beans will grow up the stake as they mature.

Water your bean plants once a week in dry weather. Do not let the soil get dry while the beans are blooming or they will drop off and the number of beans produced will be small.

Beans are a relatively fuss-free crop to grow, but care must be taken when you are hoeing or pulling weeds. That is because their roots are near the surface of the soil and can easily be damaged.

Once the plants begin to flower, apply ½ cup of fertilizer to every 10 feet of row. Scatter the fertilizer between the rows, since this will help the plants to produce more beans.

Beans are susceptible to two insects: the aphid and the spider mite. They can also become diseased if summer is particularly wet and cool.

If you are not growing organically and you see spots on the leaves or bean pods, treat the plant with a fungicide approved for such use.

Beans are ready to pick when they are about the size of a small pencil. Pull them gently to avoid damaging the plant. Like so many other crops, beans demand immediate attention when they are ready to be harvested. If you leave them a few days, they will over mature and become stringy and tough.

The wonderful thing about bean plants is that they keep producing. If you consistently pick them when they are ready, they will reward you by continuing to produce fresh beans for many weeks of summer.

Green beans are a source of Vitamins A and C. Fresh beans can be stored for up to one week in plastic bags in the refrigerator.

Peas

Children love to shell peas. There is something so wholesome and relaxing to the simple process of opening a full pod and rolling the sweet and perfect peas into a pot for boiling that it is a skill passed generation to generation.

Shelling peas come in two packages: one is round and one is the wrinkle-seeded variety. The round seeds are extremely hardy and good producers, starting early and continuing late. The wrinkle-seeded varieties, however, are known for their sweetness.

Either way, peas need sunny conditions and a healthy, moisture-retentive soil. Add plenty of compost or well-rotted manure to the area where you plan to grow peas.

You cannot plant peas too early, because if you put the seeds in ground that is too cold or wet, they will simply rot. If you must plant early, warm up the soil with plastic first, and then put a fleece over the seedlings.

Peas, especially the shorter varieties, are normally planted in a trench. Water the trench first, and then sow the seeds about two inches apart in three rows along the bottom of the trench. Cover the seeds and tap the ground gently.

For taller varieties of peas, sow the seed in one row (about two to four inches apart), since you will need space for supports. For peas to grow throughout the season, plant them at two-week intervals.

Stalks of corn

Corn

The problem with growing corn is that it takes a lot of space. But if you have no problem with space, it is a joyful crop to grow. You can grow sweet corn to eat fresh on the cob or in chowders, or designer corn to work into autumn decorations.

Corn doesn't really hit its stride until the weather is warm. Sometime it is possible to grow two crops a season.

Sow corn into fertile soil with good drainage and full sun. To ensure pollination, put the seeds directly into the soil in a block rather than a single, low row. To ensure you have plenty of corn for several weeks, put early, mid-season and late varieties in the ground all at the same time.

When the corn is up about six inches, thin short varieties to about two feet apart and tall varieties to three feet apart. You need to have space to water and feed the roots.

Keep the soil evenly moist. In hot weather, sometimes corn grows so quickly that the roots can't keep the leaves supplied with water, and as a result they wilt. Weed often and keep the weeds cut back. Corn has a shallow root system, so take care when weeding not to damage them.

It takes a long time for most varieties of corn to grow, from 55 days to 95 days. Harvest corn when the kerns are soft and plump and the juice is milky.

Recipe for Corn Chowder

On the stormy Atlantic coast of New England, a chowder has to be hot and stick-to-your-ribs in style to keep fishermen fortified. Variations of this basic corn chowder recipe, which uses fresh corn on the cob as opposed to canned cream corn or even frozen corn, can be found in the dozens of little diners that dot the often foggy coast.

If your corn harvest comes quickly, this is a wonderful way to put some variety into your meal plan, while still ensuring your fresh corn is used.

Ingredients:

1 tbsp butter 15 ml

1 strip of bacon (don't use the pre-cooked variety)

½ cup each chopped yellow onion, carrot, and celery 125 ml

2 cups sweet corn removed from the cob 500 ml (about three cobs)

3 ½ cups milk 875 ml

1 bay leaf

1 peeled and diced potato

¼ cup red bell pepper 60 ml

Salt and pepper

Method:

Use a large pot for this recipe. Melt the butter and cook the bacon. Add the onion and sauté it for about five minutes, then toss in the carrot and celery and keep cooking for five more minutes.

Break the corn cobs in two and add them to the mix. Add milk and the bay leaf and bring the whole mixture to a boil, then reduce to simmer for 30 minutes, covering the pot. Check often to make sure you are not scalding the milk.

After half an hour, take out the corn cobs, the bacon and the bay leaf. Turn the heat up and add the potatoes, red pepper, salt and pepper to taste, and simmer for another 15 minutes until the potatoes are tender.

Hike the heat, and add the corn you have scraped off the cob and the fresh thyme. Bring the whole mixture to a boil, then reduce the heat again and simmer for a final five minutes.

Serves four, but you can easily double or triple this recipe if you have a crowd to feed.

Peppers

Add to your garden staples a crop of peppers. Grow sweet, bell-shaped peppers for salads and stir-fries and stuffing, and hot peppers for flavour in all your dishes.

Starting peppers from seeds indoors is the most economical way to grow them, but you can also purchase seedlings started in a nursery.

The most important thing about growing peppers is to be patient in the spring of the year. If you set them out too early, they will not perform as you wish. If your night time temperature falls below 55 degrees Fahrenheit, it is too cold to put your pepper plants out. Even if they survive, their growth will be stunted.

Peppers make a perfect container plant if you are running out of space in your backyard garden. Fertilize them with a mixture high in phosphorous and potassium (not nitrogen or they will be all leaves) and be gentle handling them. The stems of the pepper plant are a bit fragile and easily damaged, so be extremely careful if you are transplanting seedlings started indoors.

When it comes time to harvest your peppers, keep this warning in mind. If you pull on the pepper and just snap it off, there is a good chance you will damage the delicate stem. Instead, gently cut off the pepper with your kitchen shears.

Because peppers need between 70 and 90 days of warm weather to grow properly, many people plant them in greenhouses or hot houses in colder climates. You can also grow them on a sunny patio or near a foundation wall for extra warmth and protection, or even inside on a windowsill.

Peppers

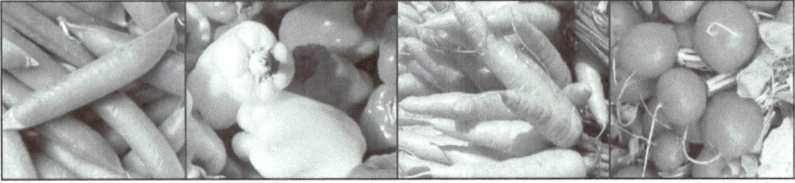

CHAPTER 5

Cabbage, Cauliflower, Broccoli And Other Delights

Cauliflower

Veteran gardeners ensure that their crops are ready for harvest at different times so they can enjoy the pleasure of each new ready-to-pick vegetable.

Among the vegetables that are versatile additions to family dinners are cabbage, cauliflower, broccoli and Brussels sprouts.

Not only are the first three flavourful when cooked as main or side dishes, but they are also wonderful served raw for snacks or school lunches.

While Brussels sprouts are sometimes the vegetable children love to hate, they can also add an element of hearty nourishment to your table.

Cauliflower

Cauliflower can be grown in fertile soil that has high organic content such as manure. It needs a sweet soil, with a pH about 6.5. Work in a little fertilizer like 5-10-10 to get the ground ready about a week before planting.

Either start growing your cauliflower plants inside or in your greenhouse, or pick up plants that have been started in your neighbourhood nursery. The plants should be at least six weeks old before you place them in the garden. Put the plants about 18 inches apart in a row and keep the rows about 30 inches apart.

Water the plants when you transplant them to keep them from wilting and to reduce shock that can restrict their long-term development.

To ensure your family has sufficient cauliflower, but that you don't overplant, calculate about three to four plants per person to have a good supply.

As it grows, cauliflower needs a large supply of nitrogen. Apply nitrate of soda after they have been in the garden about three weeks, and then make two more applications about two weeks apart. Use one tablespoon per plant. Gently deposit the fertilizer about three inches from the plant, pouring it in a circle around the base of the plant.

Keep an eye out for cabbage root maggot which deposits eggs at the base of the cauliflower plant and in cracks in the soil nearby. The maggots will be chewing on the stem and roots within a week if you don't catch them. Other pests attracted to cauliflower are worms and aphids.

Twice a week you need to conduct a thorough examination of each plant. Carefully look at the undersides of the leaves, and dust or spray if the insects or eggs are found on the plants.

Cultivate the ground around the cauliflower, cabbage and broccoli very gently and shallowly to control weeds.

Tip:

Cauliflower needs to be kept white. You can do this by tying the leaves together over the heads. Do this before the head gets any larger than a doorknob. Of course, you will need to expose them from time to time to see if it is time to harvest the head.

Perfect timing is again of the essence. If you let the cauliflower head stay in the garden too long after it is ready to be cut, it will loosen and lose much of its tenderness. Generally, it is about one week from when they are tied until they are ready to eat.

Cook cauliflower until it is barely tender and snowy white. Remove the green stalks. Wash it and soak it, head down, in cold salted water for 30 minutes in preparation of cooking. When you cook it, leave the head whole or break it into flowerets. Cook it covered with a little boiled salted water until tender. Season with butter.

To freeze cauliflower, break flowerets into one inch pieces. Wash, scald three minutes in boiling water, chill, drain and freeze immediately.

Cabbage and Kale

Cabbage is a popular vegetable in many cultures around the world. It features in corned beef and cabbage, sauerkraut, cole slaw and cabbage rolls.

Both cabbage and kale are hardy and nutritious vegetables and relatively easy to grow. Cabbage is high in vitamin C and iron, and has many other nutrients as well, yet it low in calories. Kale also has high Vitamin A and C content and one cup provides 13 percent of your daily calcium requirement.

Growing these crops, however, requires patience, since it takes between 70 and 85 days to get a full head of cabbage. It also takes a lot of garden space. Some gardeners get around that by moving these two crops out of the vegetable garden and into the flower garden and borders around their homes. Both are ornamental and add rich colour in the autumn of the year.

Cabbage and kale grow in similar conditions to cauliflower. When selecting cabbage plants, you have three choices: green-leaved, which has smooth leaves; red, with smooth reddish-purple leaves; and savoy, which has crinkled leaves.

Broccoli

Broccoli is easier to grow than either cauliflower or cabbage and kale, even though it is a member of the cabbage family.

To ensure a plentiful supply but not an over-abundance, plant three to four plants per person in your family.

You can select from large-headed varieties which have the domed heads we see in most supermarket shelves, the sprouting varieties that are bushier with several small heads, the Romanesco varieties that have symmetrically pointed spirals in the heads, and broccoli rabe which has strong flavour than regular broccoli.

Start broccoli inside in colder climates. If sowing directly into the garden, the soil temperature should be between 60 and 70 degrees Fahrenheit. Pick the crop when it matures in autumn as the nights get cooler.

Broccoli does fall prey to leaf-eating caterpillars, as well as grasshoppers and harlequin bugs. Monitor your plants closely for insects and pick them off by hand. If the pest problem is getting out of control, spray them weekly with Bt (Bacillus thuringiensis) or spinosad.

Plants that looked fine one day and then suddenly collapse have been hit with cabbage root maggots. To help avoid this, press the soil firmly around the stems when you transplant broccoli seedlings and place a piece of lightweight cloth around each plant.

It is time to pick broccoli when the florets at the end of the head show signs of loosening but the crown is still tight. Cut the stems with a sharp knife at an angle to keep water from pooling inside the cut stem and promoting rot. Refrigerate the cut heads right away.

If you are planning to preserve broccoli, steam blanch it before freezing.

Brussels Sprouts

Brussels sprouts need loose, well-drained soil and full sun. They have a shallow root system as well, so they need to be in an area free of weeds. If you must pull up weeds near these plants, be very careful not to harm them in the process.

Brussels sprouts do not develop well if they are grown in temperatures that are consistently above 75 degrees Fahrenheit. They prefer to grow in a comfortable low 60 to low 70 temperature range.

They are also one of the few plants whose flavor is enhanced if they are allowed to stay out during the first few frosts of autumn. The touch of cold converts their starches into sugar, given them a nicer flavor. Sprouts that have not been touched by frost before they are harvested can be bland.

These are cold-hardy plants that can even survive a bit of snow.

Plant them in the spring from transplants in your home or a nursery as soon as the soil can be worked, about two months before the first frost-free date. If you do not get the sprouts into the ground early enough, they will be overly affected by the heat of summer and they will bolt.

When planting Brussels sprouts, bury the stem up to the first set of leaves. Space the plants about 12 to 24 feet apart. They start out looking like cauliflower and broccoli, but then they grow taller and have a lot of leaves coming out the side. Sprouts form in the leafy axles of the plants.

To get larger sprouts, the secret is to gradually remove leaves from the bottom of the plant as the sprouts start to develop. By taking the leaves, it prompts the plants to use more energy to produce large sprouts instead of larger leaves.

Remove the leaves with a sharp knife or sheers and cut the leaves off as close to the sprout as possible. Leave about four healthy leaves on the top of the plant to continue feeding the plant as it grows. You can actually eat these small tender leaves that you remove, just as you would spinach or kale or collard greens.

Tip

The trick to getting the most out of your garden vegetables is to cook them in new and interesting ways that challenge your family to see them in new ways.

For example, you can steam your Brussels sprouts, but instead of serving them the traditional way, then sauté them in olive oil with a bit of red onion, boiled ham and orange sections for a completely different flavor.

Or take cooked cauliflower, add a bit of garlic and sour cream, and mash them like potatoes for a low calorie, low carbohydrate alternative.

Cabbage

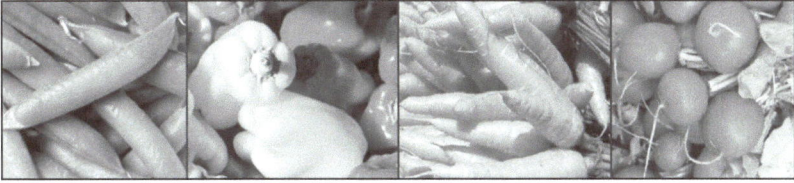

CHAPTER 6

Getting To The Root Of It All

Root vegetables, such as potatoes, parsnip, turnips and rutabagas, carrots and beets, are great to grow in your backyard garden because they can be safely stored to stretch your food budget into the late fall and early winter months.

In the case of turnips and beets, you can also have the added benefit of having nutritious greens to be harvested before the root vegetable is picked.

All of these crops are hardy, growing well in cool weather. They can go in the ground early in the spring and be left there until fall.

All of these root crops flourish when you plant them in deep, loose soil that is well-drained, but retains moisture. They do not like acid soils, so be sure to take a pH sample before planting. Improve your soil by adding well-rotted manure or fertilizer.

Do not use fresh manure because it can compromise the quality of your crop and cause excessive weed problems. Never use a weed and feed kind of fertilizer in an area where you plan to grow root vegetables. It will kill them.

Plant your potatoes, carrots and other root vegetables directly into the soil. Begin with carrots and beets, then parsnips, then rutabagas. To keep a fresh supply of carrots going for the summer, make two or three plantings each spaced three weeks apart.

You can get more space utilization by planting radish, one of your salad vegetables, with the parsnip. The radish, which grows and matures quickly, will be finished before the parsnip matures, allowing you to get two crops out of the same space.

The most important thing about growing root vegetables is remembering to thin them. If you don't, the vegetables like turnips won't have room to develop properly.

Thin carrots as soon as they reach a small, edible size. You can delay thinning your beets until the greens have grown to a good size for eating. Thin all root vegetables to a two-inch spacing except for rutabagas. They need eight inches between each plant.

Once your root vegetables are in the ground and growing, do not consider transplanting them. That is an extremely difficult process that is rarely successful and usually results in their roots being forked.

During the growing season, root vegetables need at least one inch of water each week. If there is insufficient rainfall, you must have a system of irrigation or watering. Soak the soil thoroughly when you water to aid in the development of the roots. Watering lightly so as to just wet the soil is almost as destructive as no water at all.

Root crops cannot compete with weeds during their early growing stages, so it is vital to take steps to keep weeds under control. Take great care in removing weeds, however, since the root crops are delicate at this stage and cannot take vigorous hoeing.

When is the best time to harvest your root crop? It varies with each vegetable.

Aside from radish, which we discussed in our chapter on salad vegetables, the first root vegetable ready for harvesting is usually the carrot. You can really pick them anytime they are of a sufficient size for eating, but the general rule is when the roots are ¾ inch in diameter.

Harvesting carrots is a delicate procedure to avoid damaging the ones that are still in the ground. Push the root to the side gently, and pull it out of the ground. If you are pulling out the entire crop at once, you can loosen the soil next to the plants gently with a garden fork, and then pull them out.

Pull out your beets and turnips when they are at a usable size. There is little advantage to leaving them longer in the ground, as they will start to lose quality. Break up the soil next to them and then pull them out.

The last to come out of the ground is the parsnips and rutabagas. The roots should be about 10 to 12 inches long so it is best to gently dig them up with a spading fork.

Common problems include carrot root flies and maggots. One of the best methods of control is to harvest plants as soon as they are ready. Never use insecticides on the plant parts that will be eaten, although if you are not gardening organically, you can apply a soil insecticide when you are planting.

Flea beetles are another pest that chew small, round holes in leaves and can spread disease.

If the root vegetables you pull have forked leaves, your soil is either too heavy or full of stones. If you have excessive tops and very small roots on your crops, you have likely planted them too close to each other and not thinned them properly. Too much nitrogen in the soil can also cause extensive top growth.

Many gardeners keep insect pests away by using a floating row cover that can be purchased at most nurseries.

Potatoes

Potatoes

Potatoes are a wonderfully versatile crop to add to your backyard garden if space permits. They come in all shapes, colours and textures and are welcome in so many dishes that they never go to waste.

It is important to consider the space and time requirements of different varieties of potatoes before you plant. There are midseason varieties and late varieties.

As a general rule, plant potatoes about three to four weeks before the last expected spring frost date. Prepare the planting bed by loosening the soil to at least 10 inches deep.

Potatoes grow well in acidic soils with a pH below 6, which is less than what is preferred by many other vegetable crops, so you may want to put them off in a side bed by themselves.

Mix in a layer of compost or rotted leaves along with soybean meal or a high-nitrogen organic fertilizer. Do not use manure to enrich your soil because it leads to an increase in rough patches on the potato skins.

Two days before planting, cut the seed potatoes in pieces so that each piece has two to three eyes. Doing this and letting the pieces dry for a couple of days reducing the risk of them rotting. Let the cut pieces dry in a well-ventilated area.

Plant the potato pieces 12 inches apart in four inch deep furrows. Cover them with two inches of soil.

You know it is time to start digging up your potato drop when the visible foliage starts to turn yellow and wither. Gently dig up the potatoes, knock off the dirt, and let them dry indoors, covered with dry towels for two days.

Make sure your newly-dug potatoes are not exposed to sunlight or they will turn green and bitter.

Store your most perfect specimens in a cool place to be used as seed potatoes. Eat the less perfect potatoes first.

Potatoes store well, but not forever, so keep this in mind as you plan means to make the best use of your new crop.

Potato Pie

In country inns and diners along the gentle coasts of Prince Edward Island, on Canada's east coast, visitors arrive with appetites honed by the fresh sea air and their vision filled with acres and acres of fields of potatoes.

It is small wonder then that they would be served the "spud" as a basic in every meal, whether baked and topped with sour cream and chives, freshly boiled and topped with melting butter, roasted in olive oil and rosemary, or scalloped and topped with cheese.

A local delicacy is also the Potato Pie.

Ingredients:

14 ounces bacon 400 g

4 lb peeled potatoes 1.8 kg

2 cups grated cheddar cheese 500 ml

2 tbsp ground thyme 30 ml

1 cup chopped chives 250 ml

Salt and pepper

Method:

Peel and slice the potatoes.

Take a standard nine or 10 inch pie plate and spread uncooked bacon across the bottom of it so that half of each slice hangs over the edge.

Layer the potatoes, then the cheese, the theme and the chives and salt and pepper until you have at least three or four layers.

Pull the bacon across the top of the pie and fasten it with a skewer or toothpick.

Cover the pie with foil and bake it at 400 degrees Fahrenheit (200 Celsius) for an hour, then uncover it and bake another half hour at 350 F or 180 C.

Drain the bacon fat out of the plate and broil the potatoes for another five minutes.

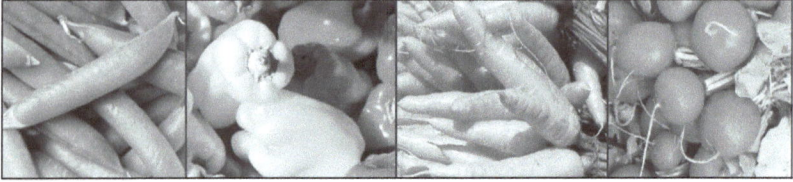

CHAPTER 7

Adding Flavour To
Your Vegetable Garden

Fresh basil leaves

If a huge motivation for growing a vegetable garden in your backyard is to live a healthier lifestyle, don't forget to leave space for growing herbs to spice up your meals and garnish your servings.

Add to that a flourishing bed of onion and garlic, and your menu choices will be further enhanced and flavourful.

Sage, for example, is the perfect companion to tuck around a roast of chicken or pork, or to cut up and mix in with stuffing for special seasons.

Nothing is easier to grow and more prolific than mint. Chewing on a few leaves is a nice summertime treat, or tucking them into frozen desserts or drinks enhances flavor and style.

When growing herbs many gardeners plant the trio of herbs that includes basil, rosemary and thyme to heighten the flavor of potatoes and other root vegetables. For home grown salsa, add a little oregano.

Cilantro is great in soups, and camomile leaves steep into a calming tea.

Growing herbs and harvesting them at the moment of freshness ensures they are available at their optimum flavor and fragrance. They give their best taste when fresh. Having a plentiful supply of herbs growing in your backyard will prompt you to use more of them in your cooking.

When growing herbs, you cannot compromise on their location. All herbs need at least four hours of sunshine a day to thrive.

If your garden has portions of shade and is already full, put some organic soil and compost in a container and grow a fragrant, healthy and movable garden to gain full benefits of sunlight.

Whether growing herbs in soil or containers, remember that they will not flourish in compacted, waterlogged soil. They need good drainage and space for their root systems to be well developed.

Put pebbles or biodegradable containers in the bottom of the pot to ensure that air continues to circulate. If you have a reliable source of organic manure, it is a good idea to add it to your compost and soil to keep their bed as loose as possible.

Rosemary

Remember to use your herbs before they flower for maximum flavor and freshness. Keep cutting and the plant will continue to grow, keeping you with a fresh supply of herbs throughout the gardening season. If you want to preserve them, cut them again before they flower, tie them together and let them dry in a warm, dry place until the leaves crumble.

To dry herbs in an oven, keep the heat low, around 160 degrees Fahrenheit, for about three to three and a half hours.

Onions

Onions like fertile soil and it needs to be well-drained. However, since they don't require much nitrogen, do not plant them in soil that has a lot of manure in it.

Onions can be grown from sets or from seed, and some from both. Sets are small, immature onions that you sow in the soil in spring. The sets increase in size and each forms one full-sized bulb when it is time to harvest them.

Growing these flavorful crops from sets is normally easier than from seeds and as a general rule, will give you better bulbs. Plant them in the soil so the necks are just protruding. Weed regularly and water sparingly.

When the foliage starts to turn yellow, it is time to harvest your onions.

Garlic

Garlic prefers free-draining soil with lots of organic matter. Select bulbs with a nice shape and plump cloves. In general, clove size is more important than bulb size in determining future bulb size.

Plant garlic in the fall of the year when the roots have a chance to develop but the tops don't break the surface before winter, generally about three weeks before the ground freezes.

Shortly before planting break the bulbs apart into cloves. When you crack the bulb each clove should break away cleanly.

Set aside the very small cloves to eat or use in pickles. The large cloves will produce good sized bulbs by the end of the growing season.

Onion

Plant garlic in single or double rows in wide beds of four to six plants across with four to eight inches between plants. Tighter spacing will reduce the size of the bulbs.

Homemade Garlic Spread

One of the nicest ways to eat freshly harvested carrots, cauliflower and broccoli is dipped into a roasted garlic spread.

It is easy to make your own, using your own garlic crop.

Harvest the garlic and peel the cloves to make this recipe.

Ingredients:

1 cup roasted garlic 250 ml

1 cup cottage cheese 250 ml

1 cup mayonnaise 250 ml

(You can use low-fat products and this recipe will still be great.)

Method:

Sprinkle a large baking pan with olive oil, and add peeled garlic to the pan. Drizzle a little more olive oil on top of it. Add some salt, pepper, red pepper flakes and parsley flakes.

Roast the garlic in a 275 degree Fahrenheit (140 degrees Celsius) for about half an hour, until the garlic is soft enough to allow a fork to be inserted into it. Don't overcook it and let the garlic burn.

Place the garlic in a blender or food processor, add the cottage cheese and mayonnaise, and pulse until smooth.

Store in the refrigerator in an air-tight container for 3-4 days.

Garlic

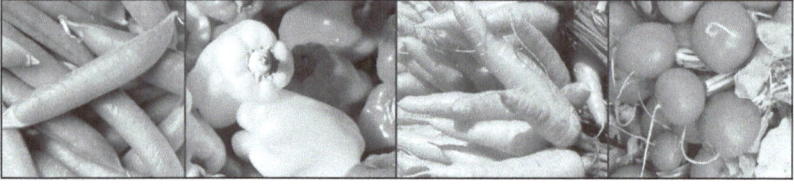

CHAPTER 8

The Spreaders: Squash, Pumpkin and Cucumbers

Squash varieties can be edible and decorative

If space isn't an issue, some of the most fun crops to grow and engage children in the joy of gardening are what many gardeners call the "spreaders." These are plants that demand a lot of space for their yield, plants like squash, pumpkin, and cucumbers.

For many new gardeners, there is actually some confusion over what differentiates a summer or winter squash from a pumpkin.

In practical terms, a pumpkin is an edible fruit that is usually made into pies or soups. Its flesh is rather coarse and strongly-flavoured. It is not a vegetable that you would eat baked.

A summer squash is served as a table vegetable when it is immature. Common varieties are the Zucchini, the Crookneck and the Straightneck. A winter squash is used as a table vegetable when ripe or in pies. Its flesh is fine-grained and mildly flavoured, so it is also used in baking. Common varieties are the Acorn, Butternut, Vegetable Spaghetti, Buttercup, Hubbard, and Sweet Potato Squash.

Besides being grown for eating, pumpkins are grown to serve as Halloween decorations.

Pumpkin and squash are quite finicky about cold soil and are easily injured by even light frosts. It is a good idea to delay planting their seeds until the soil is at least 68 degrees Fahrenheit at a depth of four inches and all danger of frost has passed.

You may wish to start squash and pumpkin inside to get ahead in the season, and they will transplant quite easily to your garden bed once the soil has warmed sufficiently. For bushy type squash and pumpkins, two plants should be placed on each hill about three to four feet apart. For vining types, hills of two plants should be spaced five feet apart.

These vining plants are not called spreaders for nothing. As they grow, they may decide they want even more space and they will take it, so keep this in mind when you look at neighbouring crops.

Pests include the squash bug, squash vine borer, cucumber beetle and aphids. These spreaders are also susceptible to powdery mildew and downy mildew.

More and more gardeners are successfully using a black plastic mulch around their squash and pumpkin plants to help control weeds.

Harvest your summer squash when it reaches a size of four to six inches long and 1.5 to 2.5 inches in diameter. Keep your winter squash and pumpkins on the vine until they are fully ripe, but make sure they are harvested before cold weather hits.

When you harvest a squash or pumpkin, be sure to keep a portion of the stem attached to it.

These spreaders can be stored at 50 to 70 degrees Fahrenheit with humidity between 50 and 70 per cent. After you pick these crops, let them sit for about two weeks while their shells harden. They need a temperature of about 75 to 85 for best conditions, and good air circulation.

Cucumbers*

Cucumbers

Cucumbers are wonderful vegetables to just eat alone or tuck into sandwiches or salads for a special taste treat.

Standard cucumbers are usually between six and nine inches long, but may go up to 14 inches. Easier to digest are the "Burpless" varieties, while pickling cucumbers are crunchier and most favoured for pickles.

Whatever variety you select, cucumbers favor warm weather. They should not be planted until two weeks after the last frost in the spring. If you are over-eager and put them in the ground and there is another frost, you will likely lose your crop.

The soil temperature should be about 65 degrees Fahrenheit before you plant cucumbers. Sow the seeds in well-drained soil rich in compost or other organic matter. The soil should have a pH of 5.5 to 6.8.

Cucumbers either grow on vines, which means they will spread over a large territory, or on a bush with shorter vines. It is best to plant them in hills or grow them on supports like trellises or fences if they are the vining type.

Dig a hole about 18 inches wide and a foot deep. Add compost to create a mix of half soil, half compost, and fill the hole with this mixture, creating a mount about six inches high.

Plant five to six seeds per hill, each about one inch deep in a ring at the top of the hill. When the seedlings are about three weeks old, thin them to the two or three strongest plants per hill.

Do not pull out the unwanted cucumbers. Instead, snip them off so that you will not disturb the roots of the remaining plants. Allow 18 inches between hills for bush varieties and 36 inches for trailing varieties.

To grow vining cucumbers vertically on a trellis to save precious garden space, make the support at least four to six feet tall. Sow seeds at the base of the trellis, one inch deep, three inches apart. Thin to one foot apart.

It is a good idea to start seed indoors to get a start on the growing season. Sow two to three seeds deep in a small pot. Thin to the strongest plant. After a hardening off period, transplant it to the soil outside. Take care with the process because cucumbers do not like their roots disturbed. If you can plant the seedlings in peat pots to avoid having to pull them out of a pot, you would have a better chance of success.

Cucumbers need lots of watering to flourish.

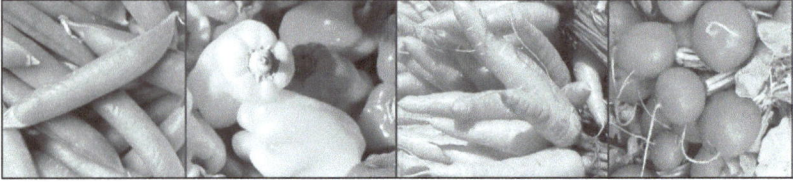

CHAPTER 9

Myths, Mistakes And More Information

Keeping Intruders Out Of Your Vegetable Garden

Most of us find it just part of our nature to squash bugs when they are underfoot and to try to rid our gardens of creepy-crawly things that we expect should not be there.

As you get more deeply involved in small garden ideas in your backyard, your attitude about insects will gradually change. When you see something new crawling along a leaf or a flower, if you are not sure what it is you will find yourself curious to look it up, rather than immediately get rid of it.

Organic gardeners know that some of the insect life on this planet is beneficial to the growth of their garden. Learning to consider the role of nature's creatures in the organic gardening process is a major part of every gardener's education. Being happy to uncover soil that has earthworms wriggling through it is a state they could not have anticipated.

But even with all the kindest thoughts and best-honed patience, there are still insects that make their way into our backyard gardens that have no good intentions in mind.

For every pest, there is a product on the market guaranteed to eradicate it. Some work, some don't.

If reaching for chemical sprays does not fit with your gardening philosophy, you have two options. One is to seek out nurseries that specialize in organic products and trying some of their products.

Another is to experiment with folk wisdom and neighbourly advice, in other words, trial and error, until you find a solution that works for you and your personal appreciation of our planet.

Many gardeners find remedies for pests through a system of trial and error.

For example, one of the best ways to get rid of aphids is to send a solid rush of water on the plants from your garden hose.

To discourage caterpillars from devouring your cauliflower and cabbage, dust the plants with flour. You should also pluck the caterpillars off the plants if you see them.

Cut toilet paper rolls to fit around the base of beans to prevent cutworms.

Shake Japanese beetles from plants in the morning and catch them on sheets. Take them away and drown them in a bucket of water.

Keep all your egg shells and use them along with pine needles as a barrier around your plants that slugs and snails do not like to cross.

Create a simple spray of garlic and water and spray your most susceptible crops. Garlic deters numerous garden pests.

The pretty little ladybug eats aphids by the thousands. Plant some nasturtiums and marigolds in your vegetable patch to attract the lady bugs, and then let them do your work for you.

Aphids are also attracted to the colour yellow. Fill a bright yellow pan with soapy water and place it in your garden. The aphids will climb in because it is luring them, and then drown.

Planting the herb sage in the midst of your cabbage and broccoli patch will repel both cabbage looper and cabbage moths.

A mulch of oak leaves placed around your plants deters cutworms.

Remove weeds completely from your gardening area

It's All About Attitude

Non-gardeners always cite weeding as one of the most detested chores possible to do on this earth.

Gardeners know that it is an essential part of the growing process to get the weeds out of their gardens so that their healthy crops can flourish.

It is part of the maintenance of life that we must all stop sometimes and remove those small but deep-rooted annoyances that threaten to keep us from producing our best work.

Gertrude Jekyll, author of *Wood and Garden* (1899) was one famous gardener who understood that there were worse things to do in life than control weeds.

"Weeding is a delightful occupation, especially after summer rain, when the roots come up clear and clean. One gets to know how many and various are the ways of weeds – as many almost as the moods of human creatures," she wrote.

Walking through your garden every day and stopping to pull weeds is an essential part of maintaining your garden. Do not let it pile up until it is a gigantic chore, capable of taking your entire weekend.

Planning now for next year's garden

To save a lot of money and get a head start on the next vegetable garden season, learn to save the seeds from your current crops. It is economical and a basis for the long-term sustainability of your garden.

Besides being a frugal move, there is a scientific side to the benefits of saving your own seed. Your plants will likely be healthier if you use your own seed, since they will have already been acclimatized to your soil.

Here are some tips to keep in mind when saving seeds.

Collect the seeds from your strongest, best-producing plants since they will yield the better plants next year.

Keep an entry in your small garden ideas journal about where the seeds you are saving came from, the location of the plants in the garden where they were gathered, and the date that you collected them. These reference points become useful as the years pass.

Dry the seeds thoroughly on a plate. Do not leave the seeds outdoors in the heat of the day because although they will dry, they will become too brittle and will be ineffective next year. Instead, let the seeds dry outdoors only in early morning and late afternoon.

Once your seeds are totally dry, be sure to package them and label them with the plant name, the date, and the location in the garden from where they were gathered.

Develop your own seed bank so that you can participate when your local organic gardening group or Farmer's Market stages a seed swap next spring. Not only will you enjoy the experience, you will have something to trade to secure new varieties to grow in your garden.

Understanding Your Gardening Zone

Every part of the earth is a specific climate zone, and it is vital that you know and understand yours if you are to garden successfully.

These zones are determined by altitude, the mean high and low temperature and the number of frost free days.

To find out which gardening zone you live in check the following websites:

If you live in the United States, go to http://www.garden. org/zipzone.

In Canada, plant hardiness zones can be found at http:// sis.agr.gc.ca/cansis/nsdb/climate/hardiness/intro.html.

In Europe, go to http://www.uk.gardenweb.com/forums/ zones/hze.html for maps of what grows best in your area.

Gardening Organically

While this book has touched on the concept of organic gardening, there are other more dedicated sites for detailed information.

One of the best is called Resources for the Organic Gardener. This website can be found at http://www.nal.usda.gov/afsic/AFSIC_pubs/org_gar.htm#toc2f

To find sources of certified organic seeds, check the following websites:

For a list of certified sources of organic seeds in the United States, go to:

http://eartheasy.com/grow_organic_seeds.html

For a list of certified sources of organic seeds in Canada, go to:

http://certifiedorganic.bc.ca/rcbtoa/services/seeds-sources.html

For a list of certified sources of organic seeds in Europe, go to:

http://www.organic-trust.org/seed_suppliers

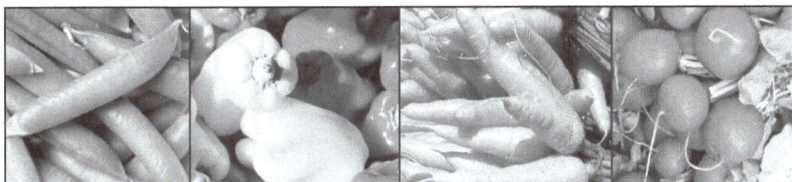

CHAPTER 10

Your Vegetable Garden Maintenance Calendar

Each season offers its gardening delights and chores

Winter (November to March in most climates)

Cover tender perennials with straw or compost to protect them from extreme cold.

Keep off your garden soil when it is frozen or waterlogged.

Check and repair or replace your garden tools.

Start a journal if you do not have one. Write about your plans for next summer's vegetable garden, or if this is your second year, what you do that worked and what needed improvement.

Research new crop possibilities and new varieties of tried and true crops.

Study more about companion planting to see if you can use one plant to fight pests that would normally attack another.

Early Spring (April and May in most climates)

Check the pH of your soil.

Start weeding. Pull small weeds out by hand, but dig out the roots of perennial weeds like dandelions.

Inside, plant the seeds of beets, carrots, Swiss chard, peas, radishes, spinach and turnips, sets of lettuce and cabbage, onion and potato sets.

Rake the lawn and remove debris from around your vegetable garden area.

Using a bleach solution, disinfect containers to be used for patio plants.

Mid to Late Spring (June in most climates)

Mulch the soil.

Harden off your plants that were started inside earlier in the spring.

Transplant crops to your garden.

Sow hardier seeds directly into the soil.

Weed regularly.

Early and Mid Summer (July and August in most climates)

Weed carefully to avoid damaging nearby plants

Tie climbers regularly to ensure they are well supported

Water regularly

Watch for pests. Keep an eye on your vegetables to ensure slugs and aphids aren't eating your produce and rodents aren't devouring the rest of your crop.

Take notes now about what is doing well in your garden and what is not.

Take photographs to place in your paper or online journal. Nothing will job your memory better in the dead of winter than a photo.

Powdery mildew may appear as early as July. Look for gray or white spots on leaf surfaces. As soon as you spot it, make efforts to get it under control.

Mid to late Autumn

Harvest crops and free or store excess produce. Remember food banks this time of the year if you have excess produce.

Make notes of which beneficial plants visited your garden. Next year you can take steps to attract them again.

Plant ornamental cabbages for garden beauty right up until the snow comes.

Plant garlic sets.

Ripen green tomatoes stem end up on a layer of newspaper. Do not put them in the direct sunlight.

Leave carrots and beets in the ground until needed.

Once your crops are harvested, clean up the garden of dropped fruits and vegetables, clippings and leaves to cut down on pests for next year. Put them in the compost pile and turn them at least once a week.

www.ingramcontent.com/pod-product-compliance
Lightning Source LLC
Chambersburg PA
CBHW051238090426
42742CB00001B/14